The Overcomer In Me!

The Overcomer In Me!

Marie Millien

The Overcomer In Me!

Publisher's Note:

The author's selection of Bible versions has been retained whenever possible. All scripture quotations are taken from the King James Version (KJV) of the Holy Bible or the 21st Century King James Version (NKJV) of the Holy Bible.

The Overcomer In Me!

Printed in the United States of America

ISBN 978-0-557-08947-5

Table Of Contents

Prologue

As you will find, at the end of your journey of this hopefully peaceful and quiet read, that there lies within you an Overcomer! You probably have overcome insurmountable situations and still yet, haven't come to the realization that you are very much the victor; even as you battle and still fight through life's waves of heartache's and pains. These words you will read were intentionally written for the encouragement of your spirit, the nourishment of your soul, and the strengthening of your mind.

The Overcomer in Me occurred as I began to exit the familiar lifestyle, train of thoughts and actions that became apparently clear, not only to myself but to those who knew me well, as destructive and unhealthy. With that, I present to you…

The Overcomer In Me!

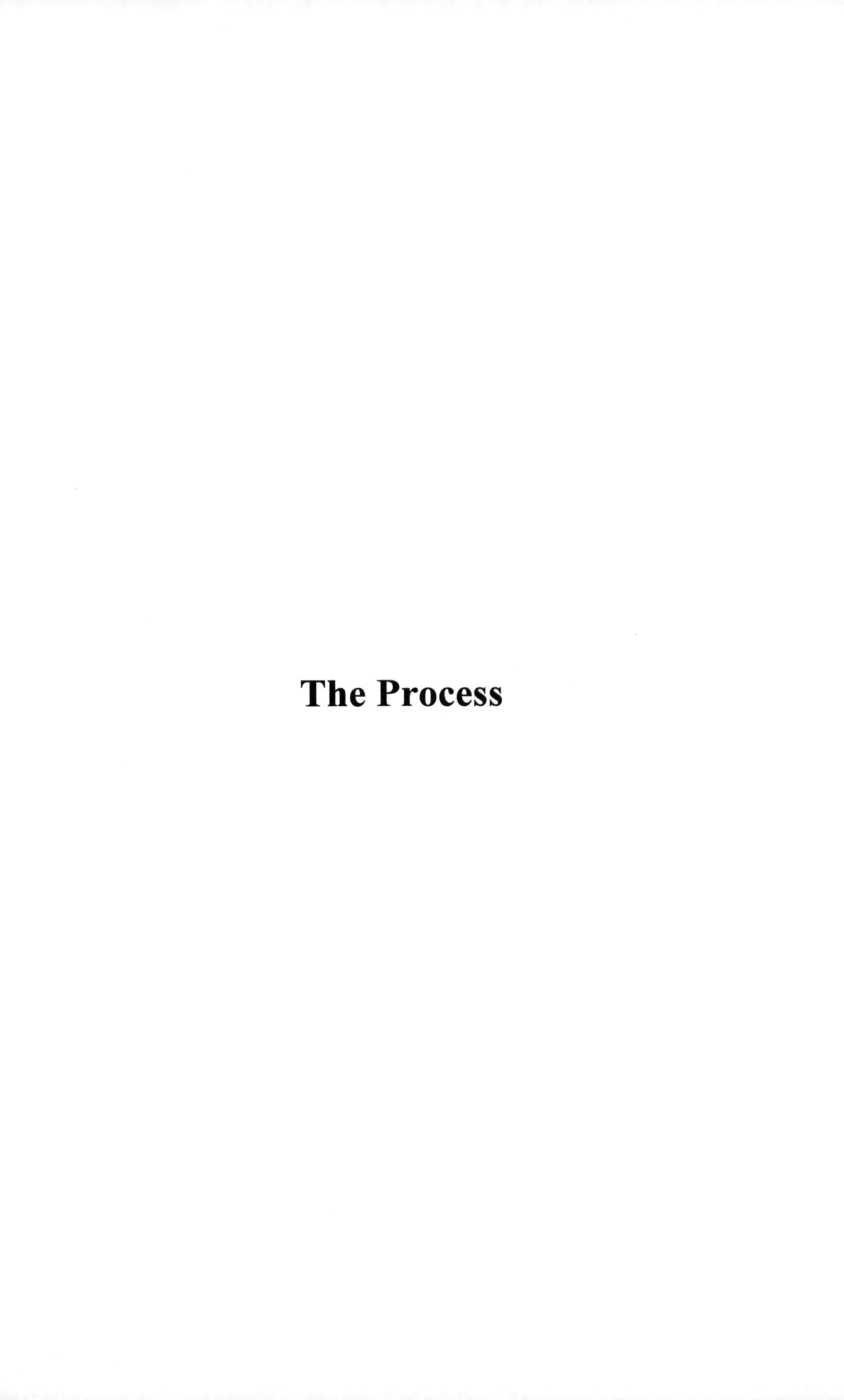

The Process

As we go through life we become unaware of the changes and the stages that we must go through to reach our true and complete person. Many times it's either unexpected happenings that occur, but quite frankly, it is mainly due to the fact that we are right smack in the middle of the process. You see, in order for change to take place the process must precede. Change can only happen as an end result of the process.

Acknowledgement is the first step of the process; knowing that we are human and are going to make mistakes. Not saying that mistakes should be planned, for that would be living in a deteriorating state of being; which leads us to the second step of the process.

Accountability is the second step of the process. Once you've acknowledged that you are not exempt, by no means of error, there is a need to own the mistakes you have made. May it be by not listening to your own instinct and second guessing yourself, or just by leaving the decision making up to chance, a family member or friends, it is still of your own doing.

So there should be no blaming of others or pointing of fingers. Finding a lesson learned in every mistake is essential for the last step of the process.

Forgiveness; the last step of the process, will come only after examining the road we have travelled. Through acknowledgement and accountability, forgiveness will take form and extends itself to those who have offended you as well as to the person that you are becoming.

Once you have exited the last stage of the Process, you are entering what I call the emerging of an Overcomer. Keep in mind that life in it's self is a process and although you've exited the last stage of the process and each and every season and stage of your life is well in itself a process.

Overcomer

Mirror Image

Self Evaluation or Personal inventory if you will...

This stage is critical, there can be no denial of one self. This stage sets the development of being an overcomer in motion.

You must be honest with yourself!

We must realize and understand in order to overcome anything in life we must be willing to be honest with ourselves at all times, and in every situation.

This will allow your quest for answers and resolution to become accessible. It insures the effective results needed.

Leading us straight to Internal/Mental strength.

Overcomer

Internal/Mental Strength

This is a very dangerous stage. This is actually where the road may fork to never, never land for some. And for others to a sound mind and stability of not only one self, but of the purpose of one's very being. Simple capability to see oneself and one's life for what it is and understanding that it is not the last stop-there are many opportunities that lies ahead for change and growth.

Going back to the need of honesty and acceptance! For without these we can never comprehend the actions needed to take place in our lives in order to reach our goals and dreams.

This is the core of Internal/Mental Strength!

It's not settling; many times we confuse acceptance with settling. Well, one is very different from the other. When you accept the situation at hand, you are therefore able to make necessary changes and adjustments. Settling is knowing very well this won't do, but accepting it as it is none the less.

Bringing us to External/Mental Strength.

Overcomer

External/Mental Strength

External/Mental is confirmation of the acceptance and now the taking charge to implement steps that will remove you from the present situation. This is an area where we all will need assistance; whether it be from a close friend, Pastor, or Life Coach it is necessary to have a support system to ensure your continual plan of action is not being sidetracked by rejections, failed attempts or just moments of feeling tried and tired.

This stage calls for an evaluation of your current running circle - those who are the closest to you maybe hindering your actions from being consistent - so as we spoke earlier about no pointing fingers, no blaming, you must realize who they are and you must place them in your outer circle; not sever the relationship but adjust it.

However, there are those in our lives that have produced along with ourselves unhealthy results in our lives that we must sever that relationship and carry on with the scars of war, for they will heal and they will be the words of wisdom you shall speak at a moments notice.

This brings us right into the Law of Balance.

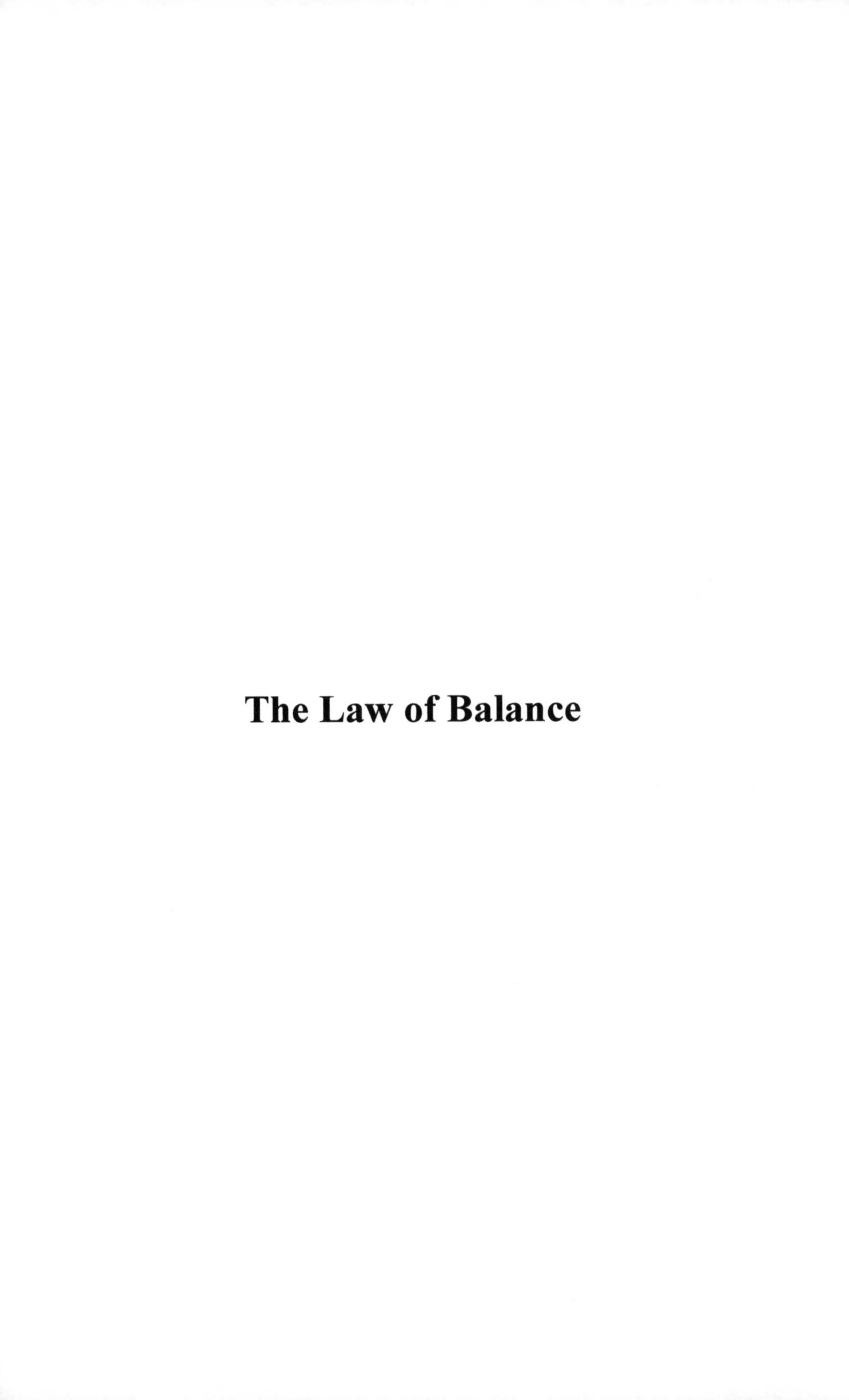

The Law of Balance

What is the Law of Balance ?

It is anything that can be separated into two opposite parts with each part having its own essence. Within every bad situation, there is an equal and opposite good one. It is your choice as to which you will focus your energy on.

Not only must we realize this is a fact of life, we must actively be a part of maintaining our balance in life just the same. As believers in Christ we tend to be Heavenly or Earthly grounded, but that is not the plan of the Maker!

We need to establish two main understandings.

First, our lives is not our own, we know that very well - it is in the hand of our Savior. So... do we shut down and attend church service 24 hours a day, 7 days a week, 365 days a year?

Surely it would not be wise - even in regards to a spiritual affair – too much of anything is a bad thing. You may ask why? Well, you wouldn't have time to tend to your family, time to make a living, to take care of yourself, and your living conditions would be out of balance. You wouldn't be able to blame anyone else, for your basket would always be empty, yet you are in his presence 24/7.

We must be able to have family time, self time, home time, as Ecclesiastes says a time for everything under the sun. We must be able to balance all of the functions of our life under the sun.

1. You must find time to eat not only spiritually but physically so that you are able to maintain the temple of the Lord, your body.

2. You must find time to bond with Husband/Wife and/or children to become a solidified family unit functioning well within its means.

3. You must find time to understand who you are and whose you are on all levels, thus spending time alone may it be reading the bible, journaling, or a quiet restful moment enjoying nature.

Second, is prioritizing. This is a very necessary stage in overcoming; it is knowing that it is okay to not be able to make every function, be present at every gathering, and that every call does not need a yes from you. It's okay to say no at times; never having to feel guilty because you are keeping it balanced.

Here you are at the stage of I Am.

These are the questions to be considered at this point:

*Who are you?

*What are you here for?

*To what beat of what drum do you dance?

"You are who you've become! Not who you were, but who you are!" - Marie Millien

I Am...

Wonderfully and Fearfully made

A Woman to take my place

A bearer of life

And so why do you not recognize me?

is it that I am yet to be set free?

to stand on the mountain top and be?

the inspiration, the laughter, the cry, the pain

Of the life that breathes in me

And yet you don't see me

I am Woman

Fearfully and Wonderfully made

I Am...

Mission and Vision

A mission and vision is not for business ventures alone, it must be for life destinations as well, and so I encourage you to dream, get a vision, write the mission and hold on to the beat that is in your heart so that you should never stop dancing, moving, forging, pressing, laboring, and travailing even on the day of the great triumph, may you continually dare. So write down rule of standards and stand by them. You are a creation that has become a child; let the purpose of Christ in you be created by your willingness to hear and obey so that it can be accomplished through you in him.

I Am...

Morals and Standards

In order for this to take place, setting standards of living is imperative. Have you ever heard of the saying "If you don't stand for anything you'll fall for everything"? How true is that? If you believe that this is a pretty wise word of advice then go on at this point and create a Rule of Morals and Standards in which you want to live by.

I encourage having your bible handy as you develop those Rules of Conduct. You will find this very refreshing and empowering. Look at the book Ecclesiastes and Proverbs. The end result of this project will reveal the hidden purpose and talents you were blessed with by the Creator, Our Lord and Savior!

Being an Overcomer is not a word that comes without work.

We are troubled on every side, yet not distressed; we are perplexed, but not in despair. (2 Corinthians 4:8)

Come to me all you who are weary and burdened, and I will give you rest. Take my yoke upon you and learn from me, for I am gentle and humble in heart and you will find rest for your souls. For my yoke is easy and my burden is light. (Mt. 11:28-30)

For evildoers shall be cut off: but those that wait upon the LORD, they shall inherit the earth. (Psalm 37:9)

For I am persuaded, that neither death, nor life, nor angels, nor principalities, nor powers, nor things present, nor things to come, Nor height, nor depth, nor any other creature, shall be able to separate us from the love of God, which is in Christ Jesus our Lord. (Romans 8:38 - 39)

I can do all things through Christ which strengtheneth me. (Philippians 4:13)

What shall we then say to these things? If God be for us, who can be against us? (Romans 8:31)

He that dwells in the secret place of the most High shall abide under the shadow of the Almighty. (Psalm 91:1)

The LORD is my shepherd; I shall not want (Psalm 23:1)

But my God shall supply all your need according to his riches in glory by Christ Jesus (Philippians 4:19)

Delight thyself also in the LORD: and he shall give thee the desires of thine heart. (Psalm 37:4)

I press toward the mark for the prize of the high calling of God in Christ Jesus. (Philippians 3:13)

My brethren, count it all joy when ye fall into divers temptations (James 1:2)

For the joy of the Lord is your strength (Nehemiah 8:10)

And he said, Hearken ye, all Judah, and ye inhabitants of Jerusalem, and thou king Jehoshaphat, Thus saith the LORD unto you, Be not afraid nor dismayed by reason of this great multitude; for the battle is not yours, but God's. (2 Chronicles 20:15)

For God hath not given us the spirit of fear; but of power, and of love, and of a sound mind. (2 Timothy 1:7)

www.ingramcontent.com/pod-product-compliance
Ingram Content Group UK Ltd.
Pitfield, Milton Keynes, MK11 3LW, UK
UKHW041904190726
13854UKWH00003B/1089